Business Law and Practice

PARTNERSHIPS
(and Sole Traders)
Questions and suggested answers

Written by Steve Norton

The right of Stephen Norton to be identified as the author of this work has been asserted by him in accordance with the Copyright, Designs and Patents Act 1988.

All rights reserved. No part of this publication may be reproduced, stored in the retrieval system, or transmitted, in any form or by any means (electronic, mechanical, photocopying, recording or otherwise), without the prior written permission of the author.

Dedicated to Leah and Barbara

ACKNOWLEDGMENTS

I would like to thank all staff from the London Metropolitan University for the learning experience and knowledge gained to write this book and choice of learning materials I used to produce these guides based on my own notes. I would also like thank the students who shared that learning experience with me.

CONTENTS

1. Introduction
2. Partnership – General concepts
3. Some key provisions of the Partnership Act 1890
4. Some categories of partners
5. Typical exam type questions (Partnership)
6. Sole traders (Brief definition and some questions and answers)
7. Final tips

1. INTRODUCTION

I wrote this short book as an aid to those like me who have studied this subject area on the Legal Practice Course (LPC) or are intending to in the near future. I have tried to produce a number of questions and suggested answers based on information from my own notes and studies which I hope existing or potential LPC students will find useful as a study guide which is based around typical exam questions.

This is the first of a series of books initially covering subject areas within the Business Law and Practice (BLP) core module. I have material for other similar books on this core subject area of the LPC and depending on interest may consider producing other short guide books broken down into other bitesize chunks for easier digestion (continuing with the metaphor) of the overall subject areas. I have not seen any similar short LPC guides of this kind in my searches so I hope this fills a gap in the market.

This particular volume gives a basic introduction to partnership law and some key concepts then sets out some typical exam type questions you are likely to get on partnership in the exam. I have also included some questions and answers on sole traders for completeness on these types of business structures. For future volumes the format may change depending on the particular subject area but will retain the important question and answer format as the main thrust and purpose of this short guides.

2. PARTNERSHIP

GENERAL CONCEPTS

Definition

> Two or more people decide to go into business together

Two main types of partnership

| Ordinary partnership | Limited Liability partnership |

A partnership is where two or more persons wish to carry out a business together.

There are two main kinds of partnership. These are:-

1. The ordinary partnership;
2. The Limited Liability Partnership.

The ordinary partnership

The ordinary partnership is governed by the Partnership Act 1890 (PA 1890) which sets out statutory rules concerning the relationship between the partners. It is considered advantageous to have a written partnership agreement which will set out the rights and obligations of the partners. In the event such an agreement is not in place, ss.24 and 25 of the PA implies several default terms that will apply to a partnership. It should be noted, even where there is a written partnership these implied terms will apply, unless the implied terms are inconsistent with written partnership agreement, or are excluded. There are examples of these that are important to note :-

- All the partners are entitled to share equally in the profits of the partnership firm and must contribute equally towards the losses of the firm;

- All partners may take part in the management of the firm;

- No new partners may be admitted to the firm without the consent of <u>all</u> the other partners;

- It will only be possible to change the agreement with the express consent of <u>all</u> the partners;

- It will only be possible to expel a partner if <u>all</u> the partners agree (including the partner threatened with being expelled) which requires an express power.

It can be seen by the above that there will be occasions when it will be practical to agree express terms in some circumstances, for example to expel a partnership in some cases, or change the way profits are allocated. This is where a written partnership agreement is important to agree relevant express terms.

The Limited liability partnership

The limited liability partnership is governed by the Limited Liability Act 2000 (LLA 2000) which created a kind of hybrid concept combining some of the characteristics of a partnership and a company.

Some would argue an LLP is more like a company than a partnership as the procedure involves going through registration at Companies House. Evidence supporting this view would be for example, an LLP is a body corporate like a company (s.1(2) LLPA 2000) resulting in 'corporate personality', partners are 'members' with limited liability like members of limited companies and they are regulated by company law generally (apart from some exceptions).

3. SOME KEY SECTIONS OF THE PARTNERSHIP ACT 1890

S.1 – Definition of a partnership

S. 9 – Partners jointly liable for all debts and liabilities of the firm – exception tax

S.14 – Persons liable by holding out [as partners] – note salaried partners above

S.25 – Expelling a partner

S.26 – Any partner can determine the end of the partnership in event of death/bankruptcy/retirement. This will probably need to be dealt with in a PA for partnership to continue in this event/s.

S.29 – Not to make a secret profit

4. SOME CATEGORIES OF PARTNERS

Equity partner

Salaried partner

Sleeping partner

Equity partner

An equity partner usually owns a share of everything in the partnership. Could be beneficial if property owned.

Salaried partners

Salaried partners are employees receiving a salary and probably limited role in decision making although may be entitled to bonus scheme etc. Could still be liable for partnership debts as holding yourself out as a partner.

Sleeping partner

A sleeping partner may invest in partnership but have little role running the partnership.

5. SOME TYPICAL EXAM TYPE QUESTIONS

Areas covered

- Partnership agreements
- Profit sharing
- Bankruptcy
- Partnerships at will
- Taxation of partnerships
- Setting up in competition
- Distinction between ordinary and Limited Liability Partnerships (LLPs)
- Liability of partners leaving
- Illegality

QUESTION 1

PARTNERSHIP AGREEMENT

Is it better to have a partnership agreement?

SUGGESTED ANSWER

If partners in a conventional partnership do not draw up a written agreement the partnership will be government by the Partnership Act 1890 `default' provisions. It is important to have a written partnership to *inject contractual certainty* into the business and oust the implied terms of the Partnership Act 1890. Terms can then be agreed on profit sharing, expulsion of partners and continuation of the partnership on death or bankruptcy of a partner.

QUESTION 2

PARTNERSHIP AGREEMENT

Sayed and John come to you as a trainee solicitor to discuss their partnership business. They tell you that their partnership has not been registered at Companies House and do not have a written agreement and are concerned about their individual liability. They are particularly concerned that they would like to expel one of the other partners without such a decision needing unanimity. What kind of partnership do they have and what would your advice be to them?

SUGGESTED ANSWER

The partnership is a general partnership 'at will' (not a Limited Liability Partnership – (LLP)) as you are told it has not been registered at Companies House thus unlimited liability applies. As there is no written partnership agreement then the Partnership Act 1890 'default' terms apply. Under s.25 Partnership Act 1890 unanimity is needed to expel a partner. This will be the basis of advice given to Sayed and John.

QUESTION 3

PROFIT SHARING

Mary and John agree to set up a partnership together but fail to draw up a partnership agreement. The partnership is now being wound up. Mary has come to you as a trainee solicitor as she has been told by John that she is only entitled to an equal share of the partnership profits. She feels as she put in two thirds of the capital in the business she should be entitled to a greater share of the profits.

SUGGESTED ANSWER

The above questions needs an understanding of the relevant provisions of the <u>Partnership Act 1890</u>. Mary and John did not draw up and agree a written partnership agreement so they are bound by the *default* provisions of the Partnership Act 1890, in particular the provision S.24 which states all partners are entitled to share equally in the capital and profits of the business. Therefore, Mary should be advised she will only be entitled to an equal share as there is no written partnership agreement. If there had been a partnership agreement a clause would (or should) have been inserted into the agreement dealing in detail with profit sharing to avoid the application of the default provisions of the Partnership Act 1890.

QUESTION 4

BANKRUPTCY

Sarah becomes bankrupt. How will this directly affect a partnership?

SUGGESTED ANSWER

This depends on whether there is a written partnership agreement or not so this is the first important issue to establish with the client/s. If no written partnership agreement (i.e. partnership `at will') then under default provision S.33 (1) – Partnership Act 1890 the partnership will dissolve automatically on death or bankruptcy of a partner. If there was a written partnership agreement then it can be agreed the partnership will continue

QUESTION 5

TAX QUESTION (OPENING AND CURRENT YEAR RULES)

Ann and Barbara go into business in the form of a conventional partnership but without a written partnership agreement (not a Limited Liability Partnership registered at Companies House) on 1 January 2018 selling cars. The business has made profits of 200,000 during the 12 months of trading ending on 31 December 2018. The partnership has chosen 1 October as its accountancy reference date for each year. What proportion of the partnership trade profit will Ann be assessed on for the first two income tax years, that is 2017/18 and 2018/19? What is the relevant legislation?

SUGGESTED ANSWER

The relevant legislation in the Income Tax (TOI) 2005 Part 2, Ch 15) involving the `opening year' and `current year' rule.

- Tax year 1 (2017/2018). The partnership made profits of £200,000 for 2018. There is no written partnership agreement the partners will share the profits equally under the Partnership Act 1890. Ann and Barbara will share the profits of £200,000 equally (£100,000 each). On the end of the tax year (5 April) HMRC will examine the Ann's share of the profits generated from the start of the business (1 Jan 2018) to the end of the first tax year. This will amount a quarter of Ann's share of £100,000 (£25,000).

- Tax Year 2 (2018/2019). At the end of the second tax year, HMRC will only be able to look at Ann's share of the first 12 months of trade noting the partnership draws up its accounts up to October each year. For 2017 the partnership made a profit of £200,000 and the partners will share profits equally (no written partnership agreement).

QUESTION 6

TAX QUESTION (LEAVERS)

Derek joins a partnership on 1 January 2016 and decides to retire from the partnership on 30 June 2018. The partnership prepares its accounts for calendar years. Profits for the final year were £60,000. How is tax assessment for income tax for his final tax year assessed.

SUGGESTED ANSWER

Derek will be assessed for income tax on his share of the profits made from the end of the accounting period to be assessed (i.e 2017) until the date of his retirement LESS any reduction there may be for any `overlap profit' if any. He will be assessed on his share of the £60,000 profits for the period 1 January 2017 to 30 September 2018 (6 months) - £30,000.

QUESTION 7

PARTNER SETTING UP IN COMPETITION

Jane is a partner in a partnership selling in fabrics. She decides to leave and set up her own business which will be similar line of work. Can she do this and are there any restrictions?

SUGGESTED ANSWER

It depends. There is no implied term that would prevent her as an outgoing partner from setting up in competition with the partnership or joining a rival business, or even if she poaches the employees of the partnership to work in her new business. If there is a written partnership it may contain a *non-competition clause* which sets out in detail any restrictions on the activities of a partner leaving the business. The courts will be wary of any clause restricting a partners freedom to compete but it may be legitimate for a partnership to seek to protect business

connections and its confidential information. The clause then will have to be reasonable as a matter of public policy. If there is a restraint of trade clause it will need to meet certain criteria which has been determined by various case law. Issues such as:
- Is there a legitimate interest such as protecting client confidentiality or the firm's business connections
- Is the clause reasonable in terms of geographical area it covers, duration (up to 12 months may be considered reasonable)

QUESTION 8

THE DIFFERENCE BETWEEN A GENERAL PARTNERSHIP AND LIMITED LIABILITY PARTNERSHIP (LLP).

What is the difference between a general partnership and LLP?

SUGGESTED ANSWER

A LLP needs to be registered at Companies House and general partnership does not. An LLP is governed by the Limited Liability Partnership Act 2000 a general partnership by Partnership Act 1890 (and any written agreement). LLPs have limited liability general partnerships partners liability is unlimited. LLPs have separate legal identity but general partnerships are a group of individuals. In LLPs partners are known as `members' in general partnerships they are `partners'.

QUESTION 9

LIABILITY OF A PARTNER LEAVING A PARTNERSHIP

Mary wants to retire from Jones & Smith Partnership but is unsure if she will remain liable for any debts and obligations of the partnership. She come to you for advice. What would you advise?

SUGGESTED ANSWER

Mary as a retiring partner will remain liable for any debts and obligations of the firm incurred when she was a partner (s17(2) Partnership Act 1890). There are ways to protect her from such liabilities. A *novation agreement* is one way. This is an agreement between 3 parties: a creditor of the partnership, the partner at the time of the contract with the creditor and an incoming party. Through a novation agreement a creditor can agree that the liability of an outgoing or previous partner is to cease and is to be taken up by a new incoming partner. Another option to suggest is to obtain an indemnity against such liabilities from the continuing partners.
Mary will not normally be liable for debts and obligations of the firm *after* she has ceased to be a partner. However, under the doctrine of 'holding out' (where there has been some representation or 'holding out' that a person is a partner) she could remain liable for debts incurred. In order to protect herself under the doctrine of holding out Mary would be advised to protect herself when retiring by seeking covenants from her co-partner/s not to be held out as a partner after retirement

(even making sure her name was removed from the firm's letterheads, stationery, websites etc).
Actual notice must be given to creditors who have previously done business with the retiring partner and knew they were a partner (s.36 (1) Partnership Act 1890).

QUESTION 10

ILLEGALITY

Barry and John are two solicitors who set up a law partnership involving an investment scheme using laundered money. Is this within the criteria for the normal scope of the business?

SUGGESTED ANSWER

No, based on the case of *JJ Coughlan v Ruparelia and Others [2003]* a fraudulent investment scheme in which a solicitor was involved was considered abnormal and incredible and therefore could not be objectively seen as falling within the criteria of the ordinary business of a solicitor.

6. SOLE TRADERS

Areas covered in question and answer style

Business structure

Taxation arrangements

QUESTION 1

What is a sole trader?

SUGGESTED ANSWER

A sole trader a person who is self-employed and runs a business on his/her own. Examples are:-

Electrician
Hairdresser
Painter and decorator
Plumber

QUESTION 2

Are there any formalities setting up a sole trader?

SUGGESTED ANSWER

No, only to register with the HMRC as self-employed for tax purposes.

QUESTION 3

What is the legal status of as sole trader?

SUGGESTED ANSWER

Unlike a private limited company a sole trader business has no separate legal status which means that his/her business and personal assets will be treated the same way and if the business fails it will not only be the personal assets of the trader. This could include their savings, car or evening their house to pay off any debts resulting in bankruptcy.

QUESTION 4

What are the advantages and disadvantages of being a sole trader?

SUGGESTED ANSWER

<u>Advantages</u>

The sole trader is their own boss
They keep all the profits
The start-up costs are low
Unlike a limited company the sole trader does not have to make certain information public with Companies House
He/she has total control of how business is run

<u>Disadvantages</u>

The sole trader is personally liable for debts as no legal distinction between business and private assets
Capacity to raise capital for the business is limited
The sole trader is responsible for the day-to-day running of the business
Harder to take time off

QUESTION 5

How are sole traders taxed?

SUGGESTED ANSWER

Sole traders unlike limited companies do not pay corporation tax instead pay income tax via the HMRC self-assessment process each year as well as NI contributions on their business profits after deducting expenses. After registering as self-employed a business owner will automatically be sent a self-assessment notice following the end of each tax year which runs for 6 April to 5th April each year.

QUESTION 6

What is the relevant legislation on trading profits for the purposes of income tax?

SUGGESTED ANSWER

The Income Tax (Trading and Other Income) Act 2005.

QUESTION 7

When must a sole trader register for income tax purposes?

SUGGESTED ANSWER

A sole trader should register with the HMRC within 3 months of starting their business (even where they have completed a self-assessment tax return). He/she must register with HMRC by 5 October of their 2nd business tax year at the latest.
Example – Bob started his business during 2017/18 tax year (6 April 2017 to 5th April 2018). He will need to register with HMTR by 5 October 2019 at the latest.

QUESTION 8

When is income tax paid on a trading profit?

SUGGESTED ANSWER

The income tax to be paid on a trading profit will form part of the income tax liability, which is payable in 2 equal instalments, the first due on 31 January in the tax year concerned, and the second due on 31 July following the end of the tax year. Payments may need to be made based on the previous year's income.

QUESTION 9

Do sole traders have to pay VAT?

SUGGESTED ANSWER

It depends. A sole trader will not be automatically be registered for VAT but will need to register if turnover is over £85,000.

Once registered for VAT a sole trader will need to charge their customers VAT.

QUESTION 10

Are there any tax reliefs available for trading for sole traders?

SUGGESTED ANSWER

Yes there are reliefs available when trading losses are made under the Income Tax Act 2007. These allow a trader to set of losses against tax under either by carrying across losses (ss 64-71), carrying forward losses (ss83-85) or carrying back losses (ss89-94).

1. Final tips ....

Finally some basic tips you may find useful in approaching exam questions on partnership issues. The LPC is a practice based exam and students are expected to look carefully at the scenario or problem posed and find the appropriate practical solution. The law around ordinary partnerships is found in the Partnership Act 1890 or within the terms of any partnership agreement (or a mix of both). You need to work out the problem posed and look at any relevant partnership agreement and/or the Partnership Act to solve the matter. The final chapter outlines the nature of sole traders which does not usually arise as a stand-alone subject but tax related questions usually come up concerning this business structure. The bulk of the LPC is made up of problem questions so it is a good idea to become familiar with these type of questions and how to answer them. I hope this short guide offers a kind of road map or basic structure in approaching partnership questions within the Business Law and Practice core module.

ABOUT THE AUTHOR

I have studied law for many years as a part time student and have both undergraduate and post graduate qualifications and have completed the LPC. Outside of my day job I have worked in volunteer legal support roles offering advice and assistance. I maintain a keen interest in legal study in particular, as well as other areas of study.

Copyright © Stephen Norton 2018

All rights reserved.

ISBN-13: 978-1729633267

www.ingramcontent.com/pod-product-compliance
Lightning Source LLC
Chambersburg PA
CBHW040254220526
45473CB00001B/473